Make a Treasure Map

Written by Tracey Michele

Picture Dictionary

felt pens

Here is how to find this treasure –
- Start at the large tree by the lake.
- Go along the river to the old building.
- Go
- Th

instructions

Key

 tree
 lake
 river
  in

key

map

outline

A map can tell you
where to find things.
It can tell you
how to get to places.
A treasure map
can help you find treasure.

This is a treasure map.

Make a Treasure Map

Making a treasure map can be fun.
These are the things you will need to make a treasure map.
- A large sheet of paper
- A small sheet of paper
- A pencil
- Felt pens

This is what you will need to do
to make a treasure map.
Get the sheets of paper,
the pencil, and the felt pens.
Put the large sheet of paper
on the table or on the floor.

This boy is putting the large sheet of paper on a table.

Draw the Outline

Draw the outline of the map with a felt pen.
Make the outline big.
Join the outline up.

This boy is drawing the outline of the map.

Fill in the Map

Use the felt pens to draw some landforms on your map. Draw some mountains. Draw some rivers and lakes. Now draw some trees and some buildings.

Make a Key

Make a key for your map.
The key will tell people
what the drawings on your map are.
Look at your map.
Where will you hide the treasure?
Draw an X where the treasure is.

Key

This is a map key.

 tree

 lake

 river

 mountain

 bridge

 building

Write Instructions

Write how to find the treasure on the small sheet of paper. Here is how to find this treasure.

- Start at the large tree by the lake.
- Go along the river to the old building.
- Go toward the mountains.
- The treasure is in the trees.

tree

lake

river

building

mountain

These are the instructions to find the treasure.

Here is how to find this treasure.
- Start at the large tree by the lake.
- Go along the river to the old building.
- Go toward the mountains.
- The treasure is in the trees.

15

Activity Page

1. Make a treasure map of your own.

2. Get the things you need.

3. Write a set of instructions to go with your treasure map.

Do you know the dictionary words?